When It's Finally Your Turn

Zakiera Sharey

TABLE OF CONTENTS

Zakiera Walker

Founder & Author
Purpose On Demand and When
It's Finally Your Turn

INTRODUCTION

When it's Finally Your Turn isn't about the celebration of the manifestation of what you've been waiting for coming to pass. Instead, it's about who you become in the process. My greatest flex has been sitting in the thick of the process of my journey and realizing that I am standing in the fruition of God's promises right now. Coming to terms with this truth has shown me how backwards thinking has kept me in the mental bondage of chasing a future that was passing me by because I lived for the next moment instead of living in the present moment. Come explore this journey with me and come face to face with what you are truly made of.

HANNAH

The phrase makes me think of the biblical character Hannah in book of 1 Samuel 1. Imagine finding yourself grateful for your portion yet being taunted by others who have what you desire; year after year being reminded of what you do not have or what you have yet to produce. Painful. Hannah took the energy of her brokenness and went to war in prayer. She left her anguish in prayer & believed that God heard her cry. Then it happened, it finally became her turn! Her turn to proclaim the goodness of the Lord. Her turn to rejoice in the area that once caused her great sorrow! When it is finally your turn, you may feel tempted to shrink back. It is scary navigating unfamiliar territory, especially when you have been constantly reminded that you were not able to produce. You may alter your moods, stop eating or overeat. You create all these silly habits that were birthed from a place of insecurity. Until it finally becomes your turn. My prayer is that you see your own story throughout the pages of this book. As I detail my journey it is by faith that I know you will get the clarity that you need as you may be in a season of waiting for God to fulfill his promises in your life. Much like our dear sis Hannah.

ON THE HUNT

I can remember it like it was yesterday, I was fresh out of college and in desperate need of a job. My faith was the only thing leading me in this season of my life. I knew God had a position that was in fact an assignment that required my presence. There were plenty of stories that met me about how most people do not get a job in the field in which they obtained their degree. In my mind I was like no way not me! I did not acquire all the debt, survive the academic hazing, and navigate sorting out my own identity for no reason. I just knew there was a purpose as to why I majored in biology and minored in Chemistry. In my eyes I was not going to allow one penny of my education to go to waste. I saw the job posting on a recruiting site detailing the need for a person with a science related degree to work in a fragrance and flavor lab. I jumped from one interview to the next, constantly being denied employment because the employers felt I was overqualified. One employer shared that they did not mind offering me the position, but they truly believed that I would obtain a position more closely related to my field, if I remained patient of course.

In hindsight that was encouraging but the reality was I needed a job immediately. I was getting weary and tired of being told no. In between that time my family had experienced a major loss. My great aunt had suddenly passed away. Without warning, a key player in my life had departed earth. I wish I could say that things turned around all of a sudden, but instead I was turned around again. I had no idea what I was getting ready to step into. One day I opened my email with a message from a recruiter. The position details were very similar to the position that I saw on the recruiting site earlier. However, in my process of applying for jobs, I had never heard anything back from the company. Sure enough the position that I had been invited to interview for was with the fragrance company I applied for earlier in my job search. I was thrilled. Long story short I got the job! Not only that, the night before, I prayed and asked that God would allow for me to work the day shift instead of the second shift in which I was initially interviewing for. I received just that. Not only the offer for the job but as well as the opportunity to work the first shift in a separate department which I had interviewed for. This was it! God had answered my prayers. First job, straight out of college, and in my field here I come!

TARGET IN THE WORKPLACE

It wasn't long before I was introduced to how easy it is to become a target in the workplace. I learned that it is all based on who you choose to associate yourself with. Without a clue, I found myself right in the middle of the lions' den. I was neutral in my interaction with all my coworkers, yet I began developing a relationship with the coworker that took on more of a mentor role. It was not hard to see that this lady was about getting the job done and doing things the correct way. As a newbie I pulled from that. I wanted to be exceptional in my role, not just a person that was there to get my check and leave.

Hello!! I was fresh out ! I was ready for the world. There were no shortcuts with her, who I nicknamed 'Bee', She always kept it professional and despite her carrying her truth of betrayal and outright disrespect, she never poisoned my mind with stories of her unfair treatment. She was very intentional in making sure I would see the truth for myself. I honestly could not tell you the exact reason why Bee had a target on her back, but I would say she and I created a bond. Our bond was ultimately helping my naive mind navigate professionally in the workplace.

In the mornings she and I would meet up and pray together before starting the day. Until one day we both found ourselves receiving a write-up. Here I was, not even a year on the job, receiving a write up. The claims had also been escalated before they had the opportunity to be resolved. Tensions rose high and I wanted to quit. No longer was I safe and I often felt attacked.

I remember reading my bible the night before returning to work after the incident and I came across the scripture Ecclesiastes 10: 4 "If your boss is angry at you, don't quit! A quiet spirit can overcome even great mistakes." Chillleee I couldn't believe it. I could not believe that God was being that intentional in talking to me through his word. Like really God? They tried me? Do I really have to deal with this? I obeyed. I didn't quit, but my spirit was troubled. I would randomly burst into tears on my commute only a few minutes away from the lab. Emotionally and mentally I was a mess. Every chance I got I would go to church and get prayer from the elders. One of them even rebuked me. She prayed the heavens down on my behalf, but she also reminded me that I needed to shut my mouth as well as forgive. Isn't it funny when walking in the spirit of offense that regardless of how justified you may feel God rebukes you and reminds you that you're called to respond higher? She also mentioned that at the divine time God would release me from my job. So, I forgave and went on with caution.

POINT OF ACTION

I want you to pause for a moment. Put the book down and address the emotions and feelings that may have surfaced by connecting with parts of your own journey. I want to remind you that what we fail to address only grows into a giant that steals the sparkle from our existence. It is so easy to rest in a place that no longer challenges us to look beyond ourselves. But that ends in this season. I speak that boldly into your life. It is time to forgive. It is time to release those who we have held hostage in our hearts and mind with hostility to follow.

_____

_____

_____

_____

_____

_____

_____

_____

_____

_____

_____

_____

_____

"

I TELL YOU WHAT FREEDOM IS TO ME: NO FEAR

- NINA SIMONE

GRIEVED BY MY ANSWERED PRAYER

Isn't it funny how our answered prayers challenge us the most? I had developed a strong spirit of offense. I wish I could glam up the reality of what was growing in my heart to prove I was more in alignment with the fruits of the spirit. But that was not the case at all. I did not like these people. It pained me to have to dim my light just to protect myself from what I viewed as darkness. This was the moment; I was beginning a journey to show myself what I was truly made of. I found myself adjusting my entire mindset. I knew that for me to survive, without becoming a victim, I had to shift the way I thought about my situation. When it was time for my review I took ownership of everything. Though there were things mentioned in the review that I did not agree with I did not respond negatively. I listened to the criticism and decided that I would use it for my good. I had made up in my mind that either I was going to complain and quit or play the game until I made strides for a new beginning elsewhere. I would apply for jobs day and night committing to filling out 5 or more applications a day.

Opportunities came but they weren't the upgrade I was looking for. In the midst of my search I was offered a position with a pretty elite company within the STEM world, offering a pretty hefty salary. I signed papers as well as sent over all documents needed to accept the offer. This was it! I was finally about to enter into my dream position and I was ready. A week went by and there was no follow up. Then three weeks went by and that's when the email was sent saying that the position had been placed on hold or canceled. I felt like I was being tortured. My hopes had been high and in great expectations only to have been shot down. It seemed so unfair and I knew I deserved better. Through it all I did not question God, but my spirit was growing in great despair. I could not help but to feel defeated. One thing about God is that no matter what low you believe yourself to be in, you can always trace his hand, lightening the burden. Shortly after the disappointment I was placed on an independent project at my job. I was excited and I took it seriously. The workload was tedious, but I remained committed. I had done so well that I was offered a raise as acknowledgment for my performance. Things seemed to be shifting. I still was on the hunt for another job, but I stopped allowing my mind to rest in thinking negatively about the position in which I had once prayed for. I exercised gratitude and I stopped taking things personal. I knew what I needed to do, and I wasn't going to blame anyone else for my elevation not being where I wanted it to be. I have never been that girl and I never will be.

MENTAL WAR DURING PANDEMIC

Then COVID-19 pandemic hit. Like most of the world everything about our lives shifted almost instantly. My job did not close its doors. It was a blessing and a curse in a sense. While we were blessed to still have a job, we put ourselves and families at risk by showing up amid our country and state being on lockdown. It was indeed concerning yet I could not help but see the light at the end of the tunnel. I believe that all would be well and I encouraged my coworkers that were on my shift to see the brighter side of things. During this time a lot was going on in and around our world. The death of George Floyd and Breonna Taylor making national news rocked me to the core. The blood of their innocent souls could still be heard crying loudly from the ground today. I value expressing my joy and pain, but the conversation around their deaths muted my voice. Internally as a black woman who is in the process of evolving from a girl into a woman in every sense, trying to process the truth of the threat my skin color poses to my counterparts was paralyzing. A pandemic that was claiming lives without a cure and a social justice situation, being radical at the forefront demanding change within our justice system, challenged me. We spent two and a half months on a split schedule. On my shift there were only 5 of us in the entire building. That was it. The week that we went back to our regular schedule, and everyone was back in the building practicing social distance, I was called into my supervisor's office. I really was not in the mood for any work drama. So much was starting to be put into perspective for me about living in a space of gratitude for life. I could not fathom anything else being so important that it was requiring a sit down. I was told how she, my supervisor, had been receiving many complaints about me and how her biggest issue was that I do not do enough. I was confused. The same lady that expressed gratitude for my performance that included a raise a few months ago was now expressing the complete opposite. This time I defended myself with facts. I was blindsided as to what prompted this. If there were complaints, why was I finding out after the situation had been escalated to include the director of our department. . I was threatened with remarks stating that my job was on the line. I was frustrated. My character and my overall integrity were continuously tested on the job.

I sat in that office once again feeling defeated. I had done everything that I could to show up and honor my duty in this position. The gaslighting and the reverse psychology were at an all-time high. I remember gracefully bowing out of the battle because it appeared that they had a narrative they wanted to go with concerning me and created backings to support them. I didn't even notice that I was under as much stress until my health started to deteriorate physically and mentally. I signed up for therapy just to make sure I was not being irrational about what I was experiencing. If I am completely honest those sessions helped save me from going straight up insane. My therapist guided me from a professional stance, and I was able to give a voice to the thoughts that were consuming my mind. I realized the battle that goes on in our mind can take a life of its own that is no match to the nature of our reality.

POINT OF ACTION

Pause. Can you relate? Have you ever remained silent about an issue because you felt as if maybe you were being irrational or dramatic? If so I would encourage you to seek out perspective from a professional. Take note of the situations that may have popped up in your head while reading this chapter. Look into online counseling if you're unsure. Contact me via email and i'll send you a recommendation.

_____

_____

_____

_____

_____

_____

_____

_____

_____

_____

_____

_____

"

ALL GREAT ACHIEVE-MENTS REQUIRE TIME.

- MAYA ANGELOU

A BEAUTIFUL INTERNAL EXCHANGE

My personality is rooted in bringing the excitement and joy into the room. I love making people feel like they're worth a million bucks. I am intentional about pointing out things that I notice about individuals to remind them that they are seen. Throughout my entire experience at my job that was the energy I illuminated up until this point. I was changing and it was evident, it pained me to even greet my co-workers. I would sometimes work on formulas at my station with tears running down my face throughout the entire shift. I was not okay, I had run out of options and quite frankly the only option that seemed to make sense was to just leave. I battled with this decision for a while and even questioned if I was being too sensitive about the entire situation. There is this narrative about the millennial generation being quick to give up and I didn't want my decision to prove the narrative to be true. I didn't allow my response to the mistreatment guide me to quitting so I stuck with it. I kept telling myself that in life unfavorable things will happen and I cannot respond by just leaving when I don't agree.

I felt strong and weak at the same time. Part of me was questioning if it was truly something that I did that placed me in this position. Then the pieces to the puzzle started to come together. A week after being pulled into the office about my performance an email had been sent out congratulating the promotion of a few people in my department. Not only that, the project I worked on independently in which I had been praised for my performance had been given to another young lady in my department. Guess that was their way of demoting me. No one who received a promotion looked like me (and I'll leave it at that). I sucked up my tears and became radical about making my next move. It was clear that my time there was up. I had exhausted all of my options and there was no room left for me to grow in any capacity. I began thanking God in advance. I knew he was going to do a new thing. I got aggressive and I started fasting. I joined a corporate fast where we fasted for the first 7 days of the month. October, November, and December that was my commitment. I went hard and didn't see any other option being a factor. I had received an invite to apply to this job. Without much thought I sent over my resume. A few days later I received a call from the office manager and had a phone interview.

I was invited to come and do an in person interview to see if we were a good match for each other. Everything happened so quickly. I went in for the interview and was able to get the temperature of the work culture and environment. I knew I wanted to leave my job immediately but I was not open to making a decision out of desperation. I had standards and at this point I was leaving my current job whether I had a position lined up or not. During the interview there was emphasis placed on me being able to come in to get hands on training with the lab analyst that I would be replacing, however, that would require me to start work immediately. This meant that I would have to forfeit giving my job a two weeks' notice and instead give them a few days' notice. Here I was still staying true to my integrity and being concerned about leaving well versus trying to prove a point. I was strategic in my decision by seeing the value in getting hands on training in comparison to being trained virtually with someone who lived overseas. Once I was offered the position that was the option I went with. In my offer letter I was set to start immediately. It happened! It finally happened! I was leaving my job. I had been waiting for the moment to transition without having to jump blindly into my next opportunity.

I cried like a baby. I could not stop thanking God. Things seemed to be playing out well. I was excited not because of the new job opportunity but because I had proven to myself that I am not a quitter even when things get tough. I allowed for divine timing to lead me to a path in which it exposed me to me. I'm not going to lie, it felt so good. It was the peace that overwhelmed my heart on my last day. I had the opportunity to have final words with those who I felt attacked me. It was such a God moment. Instead of expressing my anger and hurt I expressed my gratitude and I highlighted the beauty in my experience at the company instead of the negativity that had been consuming my mind. The thing about when it finally becomes your turn is you're so grateful about where you're going you don't allow where you've been to taint your celebration for greater. That's when it hit me the whole time I was feeling defeated when in fact the victory was awaiting me at a later date. I had won the battle. Not because I got to leave the job and get a new job, make no mistake the victory was in pivoting an unfavorable circumstance and staying with it to learn a greater lesson. The saying "what doesn't kill you only makes you stronger" couldn't be more fitting.

POINT OF ACTION

Write down the season you survived what you thought would break you while in the thick of it. Do you view that season of your life through the lens of resentment or victory?

_____

_____

_____

_____

_____

_____

_____

_____

_____

_____

_____

_____

66

CHALLENGES MAKE YOU DISCOVER THINGS ABOUT YOURSELF THAT YOU NEVER REALLY KNEW. THEY'RE WHAT MAKE THE INSTRUMENT STRETCH WHAT MAKES YOU GO BEYOND THE NORM.

- CECILY TYSON

HOLD THE APPLAUSE

I went in to start my first day on the new job and within a few minutes of me being in the office physically I was told that I was unable to start. I was instructed to contact the office manager at a later date. I did, though I was disappointed and pretty confused to be honest. The office manager promised to follow up with the doctor and get back to me. She never contacted me, I followed up with her and that's when she shared with me that they decided to move forward with another candidate. I felt free! I refused to feel sorry for myself and instantly became grateful for my portion. I was not discouraged simply because I knew that's not how the story would end for me. Too often do we think that where a thing ends is going to be the finality of the possibility of where we can ultimately go. If I'm completely honest I had no idea how I was going to bring this entire story together until now. It would be ideal for the unfolding of the story to end with how everything that I was waiting for to come to pass happened and it finally became my turn. The truth is this current moment despite how things may look is my turn!

Ever since I was a little girl I deeply desired to illustrate story telling through the art of writing. I would start and stop never completing a full script of the visuals that would go on in my head. Yet, here we are today celebrating a win bigger than any other accomplishment, publishing my first book. Do you feel that? That feeling of the champion that's inside of you rising up to the occasion. Hold on to this moment. It is my prayer that you don't allow for another moment to pass you by on you making strides to living out your dreams. Instead of allowing others "no" to distract me any further I made a decision to choose me. We are not defined by what we do but instead by who we are. Did you catch that?

POINT OF ACTION

Can you think of a time when adversity blindsided you and popped up unexpectedly? What was your response? How could you have responded differently?

_____

_____

_____

_____

_____

_____

_____

_____

_____

_____

"

SIS, YOU'VE GOTTA MAKE A MOVE SO THE MIRACLE CAN MOVE ON YOUR BEHALF.

- SARAH JAKES ROBERTS

IT WILL ALL BE WORTH IT

In the waiting period I have gotten the chance to see the heart of those surrounding me. There have been times where the pressure surrounding me would produce words to flow from my mouth that would water peoples dying flowers. I pray that you caught that. Too often in the season of waiting do we look at our circumstances through the lens of disappointment. It is so easy to become a victim when things appear not to work in your favor. Stop that! Kill that mentality at its root before it grows into a beast that works against you. You will find yourself believing that the wait is punishment when in fact it's the battleground for you to see what you're truly made of. You have to give yourself space to grieve letting go of the idea of how you pictured things to work out. It's tough. Yet we rob ourselves from living a fulfilling life by missing out on the beauty of how things do play out in the end. I did not like who I had the potential to become had I submitted myself to the disappointment of those who failed in their leadership amongst me.

Bitterness, anger, anxiety and a cycle of depression was going to be my portion had I not made the decision to kill the blame at the root.

No one is responsible for my happiness or well-being but me. It starts with making a decision, and make no mistake about it everything in this life at some point comes full circle. When things that are beyond my control start to weigh me down, I'm reminded that the spiritual principle of sowing and reaping is extremely powerful. You will reap whatsoever you sow! This helped guide me in shifting my focus from dwelling on the possibility of a negative outcome and believing for the best. Now that is easier said than done because when emotions are involved, they tend to cloud our judgment. However, the place in which I stand today assures me that my future is worth fighting for. Who you have the possibility of becoming as you navigate each season of your journey is worth fighting for. I need you to survive. We need you to survive. The Kingdom of God needs you to survive. So, when it is finally your turn, you'll see that every part of your journey was necessary. The word of your testimony will carry those who will need to hear that there is a future that awaits them.

"

AND THEY OVERCAME HIM BY THE BLOOD OF THE LAMB, AND BY THE WORD OF THEIR TESTIMONY; AND THEY LOVED NOT THEIR LIVES UNTO THE DEATH.

- REVELATIONS 12:11

OVERCAME BY THE WORD OF OUR TESTIMONY

Before the inception of bringing this testimony to life I was waiting on pins and needles for it to finally become my turn. There seemed to be endless encounters of me celebrating everyone else's turn and I started to get anxious waiting on mine. Don't get me wrong, I love celebrating with others as they journey to the next phase of life. Watching God fulfill His promise in the lives of others added fuel to my excitement concerning my future. I believed if God did it for them, He'd do it for me. I would remind myself that I needed to be patient and trust the process. Besides, there's nothing I desire deeply enough to want it outside of God's perfect timing. I want to be clear, even with possessing a positive attitude concerning the wait there have been moments I found myself weary. Though those moments occur from time to time, I don't rest there. These are the moments where I see God's holy word come to life. I think of Apostle Paul sharing God's response to him concerning the thorn in his flesh. 'And He said to me, " My grace is sufficient for you, for My Strength is made perfect in weakness." Therefore, most gladly I will rather boast in my infirmities, that the power of Christ may rest upon me. II Corinthians 12:9 NKJV.

The uncertainty that comes with the waiting process can certainly feel like a thorn in the flesh. Paul's testimony serves as a perfect reminder that waiting on the Lord holds the rest and strength that we need in moments of weakness. Testimonies are powerful spiritual weapons. They have the ability to encourage others who are developing in their journey to keep going. With that being said I asked a few of the most powerful women I know to share their "My Turn" testimonies. I pray that their stories speak to the parts of you that have been untouched.

That you find the sign you have been looking for through the vulnerability shared in each testimony. That you become brave enough to share your testimony and help set those around you that are in need free. I believe in you. You got this.

Elva
Chardanaye

Purpose Coach

OVERCAME BY THE WORD OF OUR TESTIMONY

We have all experienced being in that place where we're waiting to discover what our breath is for. I remember feeling like life was taking me on a roller coaster ride that had no end. One loop after another and it wasn't until I learned to extract the lessons from those experiences that I was able to finally arrive. I had to learn that life wasn't about reaching a final destination, but it was about who you become on the journey. I always knew there was a calling on my life, but I just didn't know when it would be "my turn." As children we are often told to wait our turns and as adults, we are reminded to be patient and not overstep, so we find ourselves in this waiting period, unsure and unclear about our next level. I made the decision to stop asking for permission and to give notice to the world about who I knew God had called me to be. There was a season of my life that insecurities plagued me and kept me from pursuing the life I wanted to live, but then I began to pray for BOLDNESS because I truly desired to become more confident in what God said was true about me.

By the age of 21, I had already experienced the struggles of being a single mother and living from a place of survival, this survival mindset robbed me of my ability to dream. Although I was still in college, I had no game plan and my desire for life was only to provide for my child. I couldn't see past the bills that showed up every month and there was my gift, lying dormant inside of me. I can remember coming home from work one night, my son was in the room playing his beloved video game and I was excited to sit with him to talk about his day. Slightly familiar with the game, I asked to join him. I knew it was a popular game that allowed you to build houses and create your own little world. Simple enough. My son said something to me this night that he didn't know would change my life. I was so excited about building my own little world on the game, I started to collect wood, marble, and all the things I needed to get started. I went to start building and creating this vision I had for my world but the game wouldn't allow me to go any further. My son sensed my frustration and said to me "Mommy, do you know why you can't create your world?" I was convinced the game was broken.

He went on to say, "you can't create the world you want because you're in survival mode, in this mode you can only fight to live, you'll have to change to the creative mode to build the world you want It was in that moment that I realized, it was my turn. I couldn't sit and wait for something to wake up inside of me. I had to make a conscious decision to no longer live from a place of survival. I made a commitment to myself that night that I would decide who I wanted to be and commit to showing up as that woman for the rest of my life. As I began to fearlessly pursue God's purpose for my life I held Isaiah 41:10 close to my heart.

"So do not fear, for I am with you; do not be dismayed, for I am your God, I will strengthen you and help you. I will uphold you with my righteous right hand."

I want to encourage you to activate your faith and trust God to carry you even in those dark seasons. We are all on this journey of life and if you dare to step into your truth you can be confident in this... you serve a sovereign God who has promised to strengthen you and help you. If you were waiting on a sign or a Word from God, this is it. Your life is not random, God created you with a divine assignment. It is your turn.

66

WE ARE THE ONES WE'VE BEEN WAITING FOR.

- JUNE JORDAN

Kaneisha King

Founder
Discerning Eyes Blog

OVERCAME BY THE WORD OF OUR TESTIMONY

By the time we are kindergartners we are already encouraged to start thinking about our future career path. As we get older, we eventually narrow down our grandiose dreams to more "realistic standards" and start to set goals for our road to success. Often, we develop an attachment to our "road map of success" and anything that happens or doesn't happen according to "our plan" causes us to panic! Before I came to truly know Christ, I had my whole life planned. I was a star student in college with plans to pursue a career in law enforcement. I wanted to be an CSI Agent for the Georgia Bureau of Investigation. There was something so fascinating to me about piecing together the scene of a crime. I was always glued to the Investigation Discovery channel, solving cases before the end of each episode. I thought I found my calling! I worked hard and graduated undergrad as Valedictorian of my class! My passion led me to pursue a Master's in Forensic Psychology. I thought this degree would equip me to understand the factors that would lead someone to commit criminal acts which would assist me with profiling on a crime scene.

I went on to graduate with honors from my master's program as well, I even got the opportunity to intern with the G.B.I.'s Child Fatality Review Unit. I was certainly ticking all the boxes off my road map to success in the order I planned!

" For I know the plans I have for you," declares the Lord, " plans to prosper you and not to harm you, plans to give you hope and a future." (Jeremiah 29:11)

After graduation it was difficult to find a job in my field. I attempted the GBI Agent exam and failed. I even considered joining a police force to work my way up to detective, but even that was a bust because I either couldn't pass the physical exam, or the on boarding process took way too long. I was working temporary jobs every other month struggling to make sense of all the years I had invested into making " good grades" and pursuing a higher education. I remember asking God, "What's going on? This is not what I planned for!" God spoke to me during this season, He asked, " Why haven't you ever asked me what I've planned for you to do?" See, I planned my life and career before I knew God, so to ask His opinion didn't even cross my mind.

God gently revealed to me that I had not been called to a career in law enforcement. At first, it was difficult to accept. When I gave my life to Christ, it didn't occur to me that I was also required to give up the plans I made. I eventually chose to surrender my will over to God

completely, not knowing where I would end up. I thought, " God, I'm not good at anything specific, what else could I possibly be called to do?" Although I was fearful, I trusted that God knew best.

"Delight yourself also in the Lord, And He shall give you the desires of your heart. Commit your way to the Lord, Trust also in Him, And He shall bring it to pass. he shall bring forth your righteousness as the light, And your justice as the noonday. Rest in the Lord, and wait patiently for Him; Do not fret because of him who prospers in his way

— "(Psalm 37 : 4-7)

After a series of temporary jobs, I was once again unemployed, yet hopeful. I began praying for God not only to bless me with a "job" but to reveal my purpose. I eventually landed a job at my current company (which is a complete miracle story in itself.) I started off as a receptionist and was promoted within 5 months to the Financial Compliance Department!

What's amazing is that my current position requires me to conduct audits and financial spend investigations to enforce the company's travel and expense policy. I spend my day finding solutions to problems no one ever knew we had or busting someone for abusing the use of their company card. I'm basically the policy police or a FSI agent (Financial Scene Investigator; I made this up!). God's funny like that, he has a way of working our desires into his plan if we agree to partner with Him, I may not be on a crime scene, but I'm investigating every day and helping to save my company money!

"And we know that all things work together for good to them that love God, to them who are called according to his purpose." (Romans 8:28)

I eventually hope to become a Chief Compliance Officer. I want to establish order, develop policies, and enforce compliance for my company globally! I can't wait to see what God has in store for the rest of my journey. I encourage anyone struggling to understand their process and discover purpose to trust the Father with every part of their life, especially when things are not going according to plan!

When I look back on how long it took me to get to where I am now, I am grateful for each U-turn, closed door, No's, and failed exams, because it all prepared me! I still have moments when I'm unsure of what God's up too, but I've learned that when it looks crazy to us, God usually has a purpose for it, so #JustGoWithIt.

Grace & Peace be with you,

Kaneisha King

"

I DID MY BEST, AND GOD DID THE REST.

- HATTIE MCDANIEL

Shanele Brasfield

Registered Nurse & Business Owner

OVERCAME BY THE WORD OF OUR TESTIMONY

Out of Hiding. I once had a steady morning routine that kept me in bondage. First, my daily breakfast, a hearty bowl of depression, and low self-esteem. Negative self-talk, and fear served as my perverted daily affirmation list. Why did I agree with these things? I am about to tell you a story of how a young girl who never felt good enough overcame! It took fully trusting God, counseling, self-reflection, prayer, accountability, safe community, relational reconciliation, hard conversations, and even apologizing to others, but she is intentionally putting in work every day to walk out her healing. Yep! The same woman who is writing this story, was too depressed to come out of her bed at one point. However, it's my turn now. My turn to experience confidence and wholeness. And it's your turn too. Remember that breakfast I mentioned earlier? Well after I ate, I would engage in conversation with fear. Fear and I were not the best of friends, but for some reason she stuck around giving unsolicited advice. She would remind me to overthink, doubt my abilities and compare myself to others. In some twisted way it felt comfortable to agree with her, so I stayed in that mental space, in a dark self-imposed isolation that didn't do anyone any good, especially me. The darkness was comfortable, but even in it, God was there. As early as preschool age, I recall having a close relationship with God, even when I didn't really understand who He was or what relationship with Him really meant. He was there, tangible, clear, visible, and audibly present. He has always been my best friend. Throughout my life I was shy, quiet, and always felt different from those around me. My thoughts have always been heavy on the comparison. Even in elementary years, I remember having scary and depressing thoughts that drove me under my bed. I would hide there. That was my safe space. Yet even under my bed, God was there. He was pushing me to understand that although those scary thoughts looked big, He was bigger. As I grew into middle and high school, so did the issues that plagued my mind. I was the smart girl who got a lot of accolades and had friends, however, for some reason I never felt good enough. Fear of failure was a stronghold for me, and although I made accomplishments, the fear was always there. I saw life from the lens of a shy middle child, who held a lot in and did not know how to effectively communicate her feelings. Along with high school came the suicidal thoughts.

But God was there, pushing me to understand that even though those scary thoughts looked big, He was bigger. Over the past few years, it occurred to me, the little girl who was under the bed, had never stopped hiding. I found myself having moments where I was mentally and physically back in that place, lying on the floor as close as I could get to being under my bed. There I battled familiar thoughts of comparison, shame, low self-esteem, and a myriad of "you can't do it" thoughts. Eventually I grew tired of eating that breakfast. I decided to take God's advice instead of fear's. All this time God was pushing me to understand that He is there, and He is bigger than the thoughts I allowed to abuse me. All God wanted was to have a deeper relationship with me, one that showed me how I could have peace and break the cycle of depression and overthinking. I've learned my identity in Him, that I belong to Him and not depression or depressing thoughts. Furthermore, there remained some work which required my intentionality. I had to take advantage of the resources He had given me. This included reading His Word, constantly choosing to think about His word over me, being mindful of my thoughts, stopping negative thoughts with

His word, building healthy community, having accountability, having hard conversations with myself, and most importantly actively participating in professional counseling. Someone in the bible who I can connect this experience with wasn't a woman, but a man by the name of Joshua. Joshua had the hand of the Lord on him all throughout his life. The specific example I want to highlight is Joshua's experience in the Battle of Jericho. God made Joshua a promise that He and the Israelites would inherit the land. God gave Joshua clear-cut instructions on how to win, and yet none of them included Joshua, or any of his army, engaging in physical fighting. God was in charge of that. He told Joshua to do something that was in his power to do, which was simply walk and trust, and God did the rest. All my life I remember trying to fight depression on my own, and I was exhausted. But like Joshua, God was there, trying to get me to understand He was bigger and could handle the fighting way better than I. If you're reading this, let me remind you, God is there. No matter the dark spaces you may find yourself in, He is there. Are you swimming in doubt?

He is there. Is depression causing you to focus on your problems instead of Him? He is there. Is comparison and fear of failure trying to get you to avoid launching out into your dreams? He is there. He is speaking His truth over you louder than any other idea or voice ever could. His truth says you are loved! He calls you friend (John 15:12-17 New Revised Standard Version), son/daughter (2 Cor. 6:18), masterpiece (Eph. 2:10 Amplified Bible), treasure (Deut. 7:6 New Living Translation), beloved (Song. 2:16 King James Version), and heir (Rom. 8:17 Amplified Bible). He does not change His mind about you or think negatively of you. He is pushing you to know and believe that He is there and He is bigger than any mental battles or ill thinking that may come. His truth is the only thing that matters to guide your life.

Ama
Yates-Ekong

CEO
Everlasting Perceptions

OVERCAME BY THE WORD OF OUR TESTIMONY

My arrival looked way different in my mind, but I made it. For me, I always knew there would come a time in my life where I would be in a space to be able to focus fully on being an entrepreneur. 2020 was that year for me. I spoke about this year for the past 5 to 6 years with a sense of excitement, of hope, a longing for more. 2020 was and still is a significant year for me as it relates to how I saw myself as a woman, as a business owner and as a leader. Grandiose dreams were attached to that year - leaving my job debt free as an Independent Business Owner making $10K a month, moving into a new skyrise apartment in Midtown Atlanta, travelling nationally and internationally on a quarterly basis leading and coaching other business owners, being able to tithe hundreds of dollars to multiple ministries and missions on a monthly basis - yes, I had very big dreams for 2020! If I had to connect that vision of who and where I would be to a biblical character it would be a mash up of David, The Proverbs 31 Woman, and Deborah. I chose this mixture of characters for a number of reasons. Reason #1 I received a number of prophetic words over the years connected to David and Deborah. David more so for his heart posture and God calling him "a man after his own heart". Deborah for her prophetic gifting and her display of leadership and power as one of the only female judges mentioned during the time of the judges.

Lastly, I chose The Proverbs 31 Woman because the woman described in this chapter handled being a wife, a business owner, caretaker of her children and home with a grace that could only come from being on one accord with God our Father. I saw myself in all of these characters, and I honestly still do. So, what has 2020 actually looked like for me? Well for one, I declared that this would be the year that I left my job at the company I was at for 5 years and guess what?! I did... I got laid off on the last day in February. In the last 3 years of working there, I started to really hate it.... A LOT. 2019 was the year where everything hit its head for me. One day after mulling over the constant micromanaging I was experiencing, I took some time away from work to watch a sermon by Dr. Anita Phillips on mental health and spirituality. Kid you not, I had a mental breakdown for about an hour crying and yelling uncontrollably. At that moment, I made a decision to construct a plan to leave my job - little did I know that I would be laid off a month after making that decision. After diligently looking for employment for 4 months and receiving no after no, through divine intervention and the guidance of coaches in my life, I decided to take on this new chapter of full-time entrepreneurship. I launched my LLC, Everlasting Perception, in June and now I am working with clients providing Digital Strategy, Virtual Assistance, Freelance Project Management and Social Media Campaign Management services.

I've been able to begin endeavors such as blogging and fitness, and launch other ventures with people I love and trust. Most importantly, I have had the time and the energy to invest into my mental, emotional, and spiritual health which has helped me confront insecurities and deep-rooted beliefs I had about myself and how my life should be that did not serve where God was taking me. Am exactly where I thought I would be? No, but I am where God ordained me to be and I know it is just the beginning. What God has consistently shown me through my journey is this.... I should be more committed to trusting in His Word than trusting in how something plays out. His Word has never come back void and it never will---it just came back in a different package than I expected. And you know what? I would not have it any other way.

Ama Yates Ekong

CEO of Everlasting Perception

"

I REALIZED THAT I DON'T HAVE TO BE PERFECT. ALL I HAVE TO DO IS SHOW UP AND ENJOY THE MESSY, IMPERFECT, AND BEAUTIFUL JOURNEY OF MY LIFE

- KERRY WASHINGTON

S.
Monroe

OVERCAME BY THE WORD OF OUR TESTIMONY

I can remember waiting my entire life for my turn. My turn to be celebrated, my turn to win something. I was always the loser. I was not the best dressed, the most beautiful, the chosen one. I can remember trying out for cheerleading and not getting it because I could not yell. I remember trying out for the Ritz Amateur night and not even placing in the competition. I just always felt less than others. I became comfortable with the fact that I may never be celebrated, and my life became all about celebrating others and being there for the ones that I loved. I became [inclusive?] and found God. God became the person who showed me that waiting was well worth it. When I focused all my energy on God and being good to others positive things began to happen for me. One instance I can remember was when I decided to go back to the Amateur night at the Ritz and performed a song that was God inspired. It was Jill Scotts 'God Please Hear My Call'. I felt like God's light was shining on me. That night I won first place. Also, I can remember when I was in middle school and first started running track. I was the slowest runner on my track team. I felt inferior to the guys and girls on my team often wondering how I had made the team in the first place.

However, my track coach saw something in me, and she pushed me harder than I had ever been pushed in my life. During the wait of improvement, I cheered on my teammates who were blazing the trails. I went from being in the back of the line to the front of the line during our runs. I was not as out of breath and did not need water after runs. I also began running alongside some of the faster girls on my team. I was shocked at how much I improved. In fact, during our track meets I was more confident and able to push myself further. I improved so much that I received a trophy for most improved during our track ceremony. I waited my turn, I did not go in thinking I was the best telling everyone what I could do. I listened, took instruction, and trusted in the process. There are so many instances in my life where waiting was the best option to obtaining a new level of success. I know that as I go through life I will continue to wait on God and trust His process. It has never steered me wrong nor has it put me in compromising situations. Only by my own selfish choices and hasty decisions have I been put in situations only God himself could get me out of. I've learned to not allow the pressures of life to speed up the process and have anchored myself in God's Word instead.

Psalms 27:14 Wait on the LORD: be of good courage, and he shall strengthen thine heart: wait, i say, on the LORD.

Hebrews 6:15 After Abraham waited patiently, he received what God had promised."

Habakkuk 2:3 "This vision is for a future time. It describes the end, and it will be fulfilled. If it seems slow in coming, wait patiently, for it will surely take place. It will not be delayed."

Vanessa Adams

Founder & Creator
Millennial Manners

OVERCAME BY THE WORD OF OUR TESTIMONY

My journey has been purifying. Think of the process it takes to turn coal to diamond. The pressure has been real. Prior to May 2016, I was a lost, confused, and naive little girl playing "grownup." Life was very dark. I had decent friends in my life, but I did not have any sound counsel to turn to for help or advice. I did not have healthy relationships with men and, consequently, I found myself in toxic situationships. My work as a cancer researcher had been draining, not because I do not like working in my field of study, but because the environment was dreadful. The first three years at my job, I experienced verbal abuse from my boss, sexual harassment by male subordinates and daily encounters with sexist and misogynistic men. I came to a point where I decided to go to God and ask him questions about my life and my purpose. He helped me to recognize the type of life that He has planned and to see the woman He sees when He looks at me. I knew that if I wanted that life and to become that woman, I had to make the necessary changes. Gradually, God began placing people in my life and positioning me for where I am today, but being on the right path has not been smooth sailing. Honestly, this journey has humbled me (RESPECTFULLY). Firstly, I have been in a cycle of car accidents and cars being totaled, which resulted in me being without a car for over a year now - in 2018, I was without a car for 6 months.

Being a woman of my calibre, not having a car and overall not having my life together has made me feel inadequate. Not having a car has been my biggest insecurity. Having to take an Uber or a Lyft from point A to point B and C then back to point A has been overwhelming financially. Pre-COVID I lived a very active life and was hardly home and not having a car impacted my social and entrepreneur life. Taking public transportation to save money is a story in itself. The people (the spirits) I've encountered have been wild. I've been sexually harassed and assaulted by rideshare drivers as well as MARTA passengers, BUT GOD kept me through it all. I look back on these experiences, and I'm blown away because now I know that I'm truly protected. My Heavenly Father really is for me. I experienced some mental battles and meltdowns during these times and as a result, I even no-call-no-showed my job for 2 months. I was that miserable! Nonetheless, this experience really built me to be stronger and much tougher. As I reflect over my journey to where I am now, I can wholeheartedly say that I'm grateful for everything I went through and experienced - the good, the bad, and the ugly. For a long time, I only focused on the ugly parts of my story and deemed them as a complete misfortune. There were times I honestly believed that my heart's desires for marriage, motherhood, fruitful ministries would never be. Similar to Sarah, Abraham's wife, I lacked faith. Sarah deeply desired to be a mother but was barren.

She and Abraham were told in their old age they would have a son but, ultimately Sarah did not believe God's promise would be fulfilled, and they took matters into their own hands. I deeply wanted my desires but struggled with unbelief because of the perspective of my circumstances. I saw my life as barren and thought that God wasn't going to come through for me. Like Abraham and Sarah choosing to take matters into their own hands to have a child, I also chose to not wait for God and attempted to make things happen on my own terms. EPIC fail. Recognizing God as a Promise Keeper is crucial for the journey. God's promises to me haven't been fulfilled yet, however, the one thing I do have is my identity in Christ Jesus. If I don't know who I am, how can I possibly bear God's promises. My main encouragement for anyone is to have an attitude of gratitude.

1 Thessalonians 5:18 says, "Give thanks in all circumstances; for this is God's will in Christ Jesus." The fact that you have breath in your body at this very moment is enough evidence to know that God still needs you in this world.

I want you to grow and operate in your God-identity so that you are able to navigate successfully in this world. Seek out Godly counsel, community, as well as a therapist. No one has ever successfully, nor sanely, ventured their journey alone.

Next, humble yourself and submit all of your plans, wants and desires to Him. Surrender it all to him! Just do it. The Father knows best. Trust me when I say that you do not want to do anything outside of His will. Lastly, do NOT compare your journey to anyone else's journey. Do not be concerned about why you were dealt the cards you were dealt. God is going to purify, prune, and prepare his children for what He has called us to do one way or another. Learn to receive the process as an honor and count it all joy! I love you, and I believe in you!

-Vanessa Latrell

"

THERE'S SO MANY
THINGS THAT LIFE
IS, AND NO MATTER
HOW MANY
BREAKTHROUGHS,
TRIALS WILL EXIST
AND WE'RE GOING
TO GET THROUGH
IT. JUST BE STRONG

- MARY J. BLIGE

Kimberly Reveil

Founder & CEO
The Kim Reveil Writing Agency

OVERCAME BY THE WORD OF OUR TESTIMONY

When it's finally your turn, it doesn't always mean everything is in order or the promise is finally realized. Sometimes it means the parts of you that needed molding in order to be whole when you get to that "promised land" have finally transformed. Here's how I know...After finishing college in 2016, I moved to New York on a word from God. I had no intention of ever living there but He told me to go and start a lifestyle blog - blogging was something I had always desired to do. I proceeded to spend 3 years going around in circles of fear, chasing opportunities that were never mine to begin with, and literally dying from anxiety. I asked God, "Why can't I just get a job and be 'normal'?!" I thought the stability I desperately desired was found in my own will, not His. Fast forward to Fall 2019, I get the nerve to start blogging consistently and my mom is diagnosed with stage 4 cancer, I drop everything to tend to her. I finally get into a groove of managing her care and plan for another start up, then the COVID-19 Pandemic hits. Another year passes without pursuing purpose. All the while I'm having literal dreams of huge success and freedom, but the physical was my same dreary reality.

I found myself complaining to God about how it's been so hard for me to do what He's said, He responded with, "You're right where I want you." In the gentle, yet stern way only God could, He proceeded to reveal to me all I've ever had is all I've ever needed. He reminded me of how He provided for me in those dark times - physically, spiritually, emotionally - and how He's been equipping me with knowledge, wisdom, and maturity. Also, how He has set up my success way before I could see. I liken my experience to that of the Israelites escaping Egypt.

They had to take the long route to the Promise Land because God needed to be sure their heart was in the right place and they were strong in mind, body, and soul first. They probably would've squandered every opportunity had God given it to them right away. There I was with this great epiphany from the Lord. He showed me commitment to Him is the prerequisite for success. - We see that in the lives of Abraham, Esther, David, Solomon, the Israelites and so many others. - After that conversation, my dreams didn't come true right away and I didn't have an immediate happy ending like in the movies, but I was left with something greater, the resolve to pursue purpose no matter what. That is undoubtedly what I needed to learn on my journey.

The glow up that happens internally is the most significant. Ask God what work He's doing in you to prepare you for what's next and how you can partner with Him on your way to the next level. When it's finally your turn, you'll be ready.

66

DON'T SETTLE FOR AVERAGE. BRING YOUR BEST TO THE MOMENT. THEN, WHETHER IT FAILS OR SUCCEEDS, AT LEAST YOU KNOW YOU GAVE ALL YOU HAD. WE NEED TO LIVE THE BEST THAT'S IN US.

- ANGELA BASSETT

Briana Belle

Pharmacist

OVERCAME BY THE WORD OF OUR TESTIMONY

There are certain life events that most young ladies look forward to – their sweet 16, prom, and wedding day. Personally, I dreamed about each of these special moments with the hopes that they would one day become reality for me. I cherished the thought of each event for various reasons that changed as I matured and became wiser. I never had the dream sweet 16 party like the ones showcased on MTV's My Super Sweet 16. In the weeks leading up to my 16th birthday, I was a caretaker for my mom who had recently had major surgery. The thought of planning an extravagant birthday celebration was not a primary concern for my family. My mom's recovery was first priority. For high school, I attended a smaller Christian school that did not host a prom for their students. Also, at that time, I did not have any friends at the local high school to join them for their prom. So two of my dreams were denied. But all hope was not lost because "at least I still have my wedding day", I thought. Fast forward to 2019. I am now 24 years old planning my wedding. Finally, my dream is coming true!

As my April 2020 wedding approached, I learned that the dream wedding I spent over a year planning would be deferred by something outside of my control – the coronavirus. I finally thought that "my turn" was right around the corner, and I was moments away... 3 weeks to be exact.... from having my dream turned into a reality. My fiancé and I still moved forward and got legally married, but decided to postpone our wedding celebration to the next year. The decision to postpone came with a flood of emotions and I felt crazy trying to express them to anyone. I was wrestling with the thoughts of if I made an idol out of the wedding day, or if my desires were actually legitimate.

The truth is that I was grieving an unfulfilled dream. Once I accepted this truth, I began to heal. I almost missed a moment to celebrate what God was doing and how He was working in my life because I was so focused on my dreams, desires, and plans. My wedding celebration going differently than planned did not negate the purpose God has for our union. Changing my perspective on this special occasion and embracing the uniqueness of our love story has freed me from those thoughts of disappointment and discontentment that were initially taunting me.

I realized that delayed does not mean denied. God does not operate under the same time constraints I do. God is in control and is intentional with the affairs of my life.

Victoria Marie

Serial Entrepreneur & Wealth Strategist

My relationship with God had gone to another level. I enjoyed each lesson He taught me. It was so divine. One day, I realized I was barely getting by. I'll never forget my prayer to God. It went something like this, "God, I want to do more than just survive, I want to thrive. I'm tired of being broke." At that moment God taught me a valuable lesson about the power of my words. He began to teach me that I have to be intentional about my word choice. He showed me that my negative words were canceling out what He was trying to do for me. I can't speak both blessing and curses. I was telling God that I wanted to thrive but in the same breath I called myself broke. You may be thinking, what's the big deal? Well, there's so much power in our words. So often we freely use our tongues because we don't acknowledge the authority our words hold. This lesson was life changing. From that point on, I was very intentional about the words I allowed out of my mouth. Two weeks later, I ended up meeting a young man. I remember that day like it was yesterday. I was at Five Points getting a pedicure at City Nails. I was extremely frustrated because I had to wait in line for so long.

Mainly, I was frustrated because I had to pay for parking, and it was going to expire soon. I finally get in the chair and then boom, my nail lady, T, drops my phone in the water. I was overwhelmed and really wanted to cry. I was making $150 a week at the time, and I couldn't afford another phone. After T got done with my nails, I ran out to my car trying to beat the parking attendant before he booted my car. The Lord knew that that would have been my breaking point. As I'm running to my car, this guy pulls up in a matte white BMW trying to holler. Honestly, I was not having it at first. I was just trying to avoid getting booted, but this man was so persistent. Finally, I caved in and gave him my Instagram and in exchange he gave me his business card. Long story short, he became my boyfriend and he later introduced me to an opportunity to make money. My first week of working with him, I made what I made in one week, in one hour. I was shook and excited. I went from making about 12,000 yearly to six figures. My tax bracket changed and so did my circle. God began to expose me to people who were doing financially well. It was in this exposure I started to desire a lifestyle I knew nothing about. About two years later, the guy and I had a nasty breakup. He told me I was fired. I was so scared.

I didn't have a degree and the only thing I was for sure good at was serving. Now, my prayer to God. shifted. "God, can you be my CEO? I don't like having my livelihood in the hands of others." About two weeks later, the law firm I was contracted with asked if I wanted to continue working with them. They told me I was the best at the firm. I began crying because God had answered my prayer years ago, but I needed a shift in perspective to recognize it. That day marked the day of my entrepreneurship journey with God being my CEO. Waiting on God is simple but isn't always the easiest thing to do. God's words that were spoken to me in my darkest days took 5 years to manifest. However, it was a season necessary for shaping me and molding me for this time. If you are reading this book, I wholeheartedly believe that it is finally your turn. I'm reminded of a passage in John 2. When Jesus was at a wedding and they ran out of wine. Mary asked Jesus to make more. Jesus' response was "My time has not yet come" (John 2:4). I was surprised at Jesus' response, but even more at Mary's. She completely disregarded

His statement. She told the servants to do whatever Jesus tells them.

You may feel inadequate, unprepared, or unable but your obedience will make room for you. Mary already knew the importance of obeying God. Notice she did not even question how He was going to do it, she just told the servants to do what He says. I want to leave you with this, do whatever God commands you to do. Staying in the will of God is your protection. There is a problem out there that God has called you to be an answer to, but you must trust and obey. Open your eyes and hearts. It is finally your turn.

Roxanne A. Charles, J.D.

OVERCAME BY THE WORD OF OUR TESTIMONY

For as long as I can remember I've wanted to be a lawyer. There's something about defending the weak and fighting for justice that sets me on fire! My journey to J.D. began in 1996 when my Freshman year of college came to a screeching halt as I suffered an injury at the hands of a coworker that I'd have to heal from for the rest of my life. I was able to begin school again the following year, but a second emergency surgery set me back once again. Over the next few years recovering from the injury, working, and marriage headed my agenda. Then, in 2002 the unexpected happened. My husband was deported! Here I was a young lady trying to find my groove in life but I kept getting knocked down. I worried my dream would never be realized. Two years pass and I'm able to start school again. I graduate with a Bachelor's of Arts in Legal Studies. Yes, I'm finally on my way! Praise God! I begin applications for law school, and boom, my father falls ill. I became his primary caretaker and my path to law school is halted yet again! Unfortunately, my dad passed away in 2013, that took an enormous toll on me mentally, physically, and spiritually.

I focused on working and promised myself one day I'd start progressing toward law school again. Little did I know I'd have a jumpstart the following year. On the job a coworker, who I'd seldom crossed paths with opened a harassment case against me. This totally came out of left field because, as stated, I very rarely, if ever, interacted with this person! Like I shared, fighting for justice sets me on fire - fair treatment for all is the fuel that energizes me daily. By the grace of God the false accusations were unfounded. I knew there was no way I could continue on without the tools to uphold justice at full capacity.

So, I applied for law school and I got in! Hallelujah! I'm finally living the dream when just a year into my schooling my mother falls ill. I think, "Not again, Lord!" I couldn't go through the same situation I did with my father. I made it through the first semester of school but with the added stress of my mom's illness, I faced academic dismissal. I was DEVASTATED. In fact, devastated is an understatement. I felt like the rug had been pulled out from under yet again. As my mom healed, I decided to obtain my paralegal certification. I thought, "If I can't be a lawyer yet, I'll get as close as possible!" The next year I applied to a new school, The Charleston School of Law in South Carolina, and got admitted!

Yes! By God's strength, I make it all the way through my third year.

I recited Psalm 138:8, "The Lord will fulfill his promise for me; your steadfast love, O Lord, endures forever. Do not forsake the work of your hands."

At the end of my second year in law school my sister was diagnosed with stage 4 metastatic colon cancer. That was a blow to the stomach that still haunts me. I fought back tears during classes, overwhelmed at the thought of losing my only sister and worried I wouldn't experience the victory I was so close I could taste. I cried out to God, "Please help me! This is too much!" He gifted me with endurance, perseverance, and faith to make it through. The beginning of 2020 comes and I'm gearing up to finish my last semester when I suddenly suffer an injury causing three herniated discs in my neck. I endured excruciating pain and agony I wouldn't wish on my worst enemy.

I pray, "God, I'm SO CLOSE! Please just let me finish!" He

replied, "I will fulfill my promise to you." He did just that. On November 20, 2020 I was pinned Juris Doctor.

Who would've imagined my journey to becoming a lawyer would stretch beyond 20 years. The long, winding road led to it finally being my turn to live the dream. I echo the words in Revelation 14:12 to you, "Here is a call for endurance for the saints, those who keep the commandments of God and have their faith in Jesus."

If your journey is full of setbacks and potholes and brick walls, endure! Remember Philippians 1:4-6, "He who began a good work in you will bring it to completion." When it's finally your turn you'll be able to stand strong and firm, flying proudly the banner of victory from the Lord your God.

Roxanne A. Charles, J.D.

"

NOTHING --- NOTHING IS TOO FAR GONE THAT GOD CANNOT RESURRECT IT.

- PRISCILLA SHIRER

Arnesjah Miller

Founder
Transparent Treasure

OVERCAME BY THE WORD OF OUR TESTIMONY

I was watching a Facebook LIVE video one evening by a well-known leader that I follow. Towards the end of her message, she randomly gave a prophetic word to various people who were watching. I was intrigued by God speaking through her, so I decided to watch until the very end. She mentioned, "I feel this one strongly within me! Someone is supposed to be releasing a book. But you've been afraid!" My eyes opened wide. My body immediately went into shock with heat running all over me. I had been contemplating releasing my book, "I...Am Chosen: 21 Biblical Affirmations to Develop Your God-Identity", either in the current year (2019) or the next year (2020). She continued to release the prophetic word which resonated completely with my life. Tears streamed down my face as I sent a voice message to my friend who was helping me edit the book, "I'm supposed to release my book this year. I have to. I just heard a prophetic word confirming that it has to happen this year!" I was contemplating the release date of my book because I felt I wasn't ready to take on the assignment. I already knew the pressure that came with it.

I knew the challenges I'd face. I wanted to remain hidden. Even though I'd written about being chosen by God to step into your purpose, I was the one who wanted to hide under a rock instead. Sounds crazy right? But that's how you know that God is using you to fulfill His will. It is not in your own strength that the task will get completed, it is God working through you to fulfill the task. When it was my turn, I had no choice but to step out on faith. I published I...Am Chosen December 8, 2019 trusting that God would do something great with it. I had no goal in mind. I just ordered 200 books to sell in person with an attempt to be prepared. I imagined 200 people coming up to me to purchase my book, but God had other plans. It was my turn to step out to meet with others. It wasn't the time to stay shut in doors to hope for miracles. It was time to go out and let my voice be heard; to share with someone in the world that God has a purpose and plan for their lives because they are chosen. One day I felt a strong tug in my heart to begin going to various malls in North Atlanta to share my book with others. My first attempt was not successful at Phipps Plaza, a mall well-known for its high-end fashion. At the time, the people and environment seemed too intimidating for me and I felt too little to be of any importance to them.

I tried again another day. I went to various malls in Atlanta on different days where I actually handed out free bookmarks to people to create conversation and talk about my book. Then finally one day, I arrived at Cumberland Mall. Walking out of Charlotte Russe, I came across the Sleep is 4 Suckers kiosk where I saw a familiar face - Jamel Jackson - who is partnered with Sleep is 4 Suckers. We held small talk. I told him about my book and he asked if I would like to volunteer in selling Sleep is 4 Suckers products as well as his book. It didn't take long for me to accept the opportunity. Volunteering turned into working for him. 6 months later, working for him turned into an opportunity for me to sell my books with them for 3 months, which in return brought leverage for my brand. One year later, I...Am Chosen has reached the hands of over 700 people leading me into making over $15,000 in revenue. I've received feedback stating how much I...Am Chosen has impacted lives. In one book alone, God moved upon the hearts of others to make a change in their lives; to stand up to pursue their purpose, and to embrace their God-identity. As a result, answering the call to step further into my purpose is to inspire others to arise when it is their turn. No matter how scary your calling appears to be.

There comes a time where you have to do what you are called to do even though you are afraid. God knows how much you can handle and He will provide step after step. The outcome of your obedience is beyond your imagination. So, do it afraid, beloved. The leap isn't so scary after all.

66

I TRULY BELIEVE THAT IF YOU PUT YOUR GOALS IN WRITING, SPEAK THEM OUT LOUD, AND WORK FOR THEM, THEY WILL HAPPEN

- CIARA

Tasha Askew

Founder
Soul Healing Experience (S.H.E)

I'm reminded of the words Christ spoke in John 2:4, when He said to his mom, "Dear woman, that's not our problem. My time has not yet come."

At this point, we zoom in on Christ, his mother, and their friends at a wedding. The bride and groom have run into a dilemma & they are completely out of wine to serve their guests. In an effort to help them out, Mary, Christ's mother suggests He do something to solve the problem. Instead, Christ says, "His time has not come yet." Within a matter of moments, it suddenly becomes His "time" because herein is where we see Him perform His very first miracle. When Christ's "turn came" it was a moment for Him to surrender to what God had planned to do through Him at the wedding - perform the first miracle. When Christ's "turn came" it was a moment for Him to surrender to what God had planned to do through Him at the wedding - perform the first miracle. When "my turn" came, it was for me to surrender to what Abba had planned to do through me - teach His Children His Word. In essence, my turn was simply a moment to "surrender." Over the years, I've gained clarity that "my turn" is really a misnomer.

"My turn" is synonymous with His turn, because it becomes an opportunity for us to release a unique expression of His glory. Many times we struggle to be seen. We struggle with wanting our few ethereal minutes of fame. Only to come to the conclusion that what we truly desire is a climatic release of the treasure that has been placed on the inside of us since conception.

"But we have this treasure in jars of clay to show that this all-surpassing power is from God and not from us." 2 Corinthians 4:7

This is where true joy rests. It's that sweet spot of allowing His will to be done on Earth as it is in Heaven through the vessel that is...YOU. When it's your turn, surrender to His perfect plan to be released through you.

-Tasha Askew

@tashateachestruth

66

SOMETIMES PEOPLE
TRY TO DESTROY
YOU, PERCISELY
BECAUSE THEY
RECOGNIZE YOUR
POWER NOT
BECAUSE THEY
DON'T SEE IT. BUT
BECAUSE THEY SEE
IT AND THEY DON'T
WANT IT TO EXIST

- BELL HOOKS

POINT OF ACTION

Your Turn! what's the beauty that's illustrated by the words of your testimony?

_____

_____

_____

_____

_____

_____

_____

_____

_____

_____

BONUS: (When It's Finally Your Turn: Love Edition)

I pray that when a love finally comes into your life that chooses you that you will find strength inside yourself that is greater than the fear of the past & you decide to choose it back! No matter how scary or how much it seems too good to be true. You deserve it! ♥ In the meantime, work on YOU for YOU!

"

DON'T EVER STOP. KEEP GOING. IF YOU WANT A TASTE OF FREEDOM, KEEP GOING.

- HARRIET TUBMAN

ZAKIERA WALKER